The

Ex Recovery Blueprint

The Quickest Way to Get Your Ex Back Guaranteed!

By Zac Miller

Table of Contents

Disclaimer

This book is written for entertainment and informational purposes only. This book should be used in the making of an informed decision only. The publisher and author shall have neither liability nor responsibility to any person or entity with respect to any loss or damage caused or alleged to be caused directly or indirectly by this book. This book is in no way affiliated with Facebook, Snapchat, Tinder, or any other app or website.

STOP

You have been broken up with and you want your ex back. You need to hold everything, and read this entire book before you make your next move.

Introduction

If you are reading this right now you are probably hurting. You've been broken up with by someone you loved and cared about deeply. The cause of the break up is irrelevant right now; the relationship ended and you want to reunite with your ex. I commend you for making the effort to get your ex back properly, as this will greatly benefit you.

Sometimes our partners don't make sense when they break up with us. They may have said one thing but meant another. In this book, I will explain the most common reasons relationships end, and how to properly get your ex back and keep them for the long run. This book is extensive, but to the point. Make sure you read the entire book before you do anything, as you must understand all the information contained to make this process work.

Some readers of this book may decide they want extra help, or find themselves in a unique break-up situation. For this reason, I offer a *VIP Relationship Coaching* section on my website, which can be found at GetMoreDates.com. This is available to both males and females. If you do decide to reach out to me, I first want you to read this entire book and understand the information contained. This is very important, as you need to understand my entire philosophy of how you are to get your ex back.

Note: (During this book the boyfriends name will be Robert, and the girlfriends name Jessica. They are just example names.)

Chapter #1
Why Did They Break Up With Me

_____

Before you even think of getting back with your ex, you have to answer this question... why did they break up with you? Unfortunately your ex will never give you a direct answer and probably said something like, "We just grew apart," or "I just want to be single right now." But you're lucky, you have me! I just want you to remember that yes, they did break up with you... but they also dated you. This indicates that they had feelings for you... feelings that you can get back! You're not just gone in an instant and are still in their mind. First and foremost, here are the things you need to stop doing right away!

- *Telling your ex you love them*
- *Buying your ex gifts*
- *Telling your ex you'll change*
- *Calling them*
- *Texting them*

- *"Accidentally" bumping into them*
- *Begging them*
- *Trying to reason with them*
- *Apologizing to them*

There is no line that will instantly bring an ex back and all of the techniques above actually PUSH your ex away... and away into the arms of someone else if you're unlucky. There's a famous quote which goes, "Why would you keep doing the same thing if it didn't work the first hundred times?" Think about it, if you apologized 100 times, do you really think that on 101 your ex will come back? You have to realize something, it's more than apologies and gifts with relationships. People do not always think logically, especially when it comes to relationships; they run on emotions! With that being said, you cannot reason with an ex-partner on why you both should be together.

Let's think about this, many times men and women complain about how their partners are such jerks and ass holes, yet they stay with them! Why is that you ask? It's because the attraction they feel for them outweighs the negative qualities that they don't like. You see it's the attraction your ex felt for you that went away, which is most likely the reason a break up occurred. So take a seat student, because you just signed up for Attraction 101 and I'm your professor, Zac Miller.

<u>Attraction</u>

For both sexes, the main aspects of attraction are looks and personality. However, there are a number of other qualities which go along with looks and personality that also make someone feel attracted to you. Let's go over qualities that **attract** the opposite sex:

- **Leadership** - You take control of the situation. You decide where dinner will be, what song you're going to listen to, and what you're going to wear; you take the lead. This trait is more important for men.

- **Confidence** - It's the universal quality that attracts both men and women, confidence. Who wants to date an insecure wussbag? You guessed it, no one.

- **Self-Esteem** - This ties into confidence but is a little different. As you may be confident in certain situations, how you feel about yourself will show. No one wants to sit around babying their partner.

- **Purpose** - Your goals, your desires, your passions. Where you're going, and what you dream to do. You should have a purpose. This is a big one which we will go over more later in the book.

- **Challenge** - Everyone likes a little bit of a chase, even in long-term relationships. It's okay to sometimes make your partner miss you, or to not say "yes" to their every wish. Being a little bit of a challenge breeds attraction.

- **Looks -** Of course how you look is a big factor if someone is attracted to you. Everyone wants their partner to look good! So get a new hair style, wear some nice clothes, make sure you smell nice, whiten your teeth, and just do whatever need to in order to look the best you can.

So if those are some qualities that attract the opposite sex, what is the opposite sex un-attracted to? Well pretty much the exact opposites. Here are negative qualities that people find *unattractive*:

- **Jealousy** - Jealousy is never attractive. Some people will play games to try to make their partner jealous, but the more you remain unphased, the more attractive you look. Now you don't want to sit around and get walked on so there are situations where you need to confront your partner, such as if they are talking to their ex. But if somebody of the opposite sex messages your partner on Facebook saying hi and you flip out, this is a problem.

- **Being Controlling** - Your partner has a life too. Though people love when you control the relationship, they don't want you to control their life; big turn off.

- **Not Valuing Yourself/Putting Your Partner on a Pedestal** - When you are always putting them 1st, and yourself 2nd, it does not make for a good relationship. Partners should be equal in a relationship.

- **Being Clingy** - If you are texting and calling them all day, asking to hang out constantly, and feel you are always initiating everything, you are being a clinger! No girl or guy wants to be smothered by their partner.

- **Being Approval Seeking** - It's okay once in a while but if you're asking your girlfriend or boyfriend for approval on every decision you make, approval seeking becomes a problem.

Now you may not be displaying all the negative qualities I mention on the list above, but you may be displaying some of them. Let me give you a brief overview of what usually happens when relationships end and see if you can relate to it.

At the beginning of the relationship you portray all the positive qualities from the list before: you have a purpose, you're confident, and so much more. As the relationship develops, something changes, which becomes the ultimate reason the break up occurs. Maybe you started portraying some of the unattractive qualities mentioned before, such as being jealous, clingy, controlling, etc. You may have started putting all your hobbies, interests, friends, and goals second, and your partner first. You may have gotten mad when your partner wanted to hang out with their friends. Maybe you asked for their approval before you did anything. You could have started smothering your partner, trying to be with them every moment of the day. And then you might have started to allow them to have all the control.

Golden Rule

The golden rule in any relationship is "the person who cares the least controls the relationship." It's not a nice rule, but it is true. You have more control, as long as you seem like you care less.

Once these changes started taking place, your partner's interest level began declining. As I said before, looks are one thing but personality is the biggest factor to the opposite sex! Something changed, which is why your partner broke up with you. Most likely, you're not the same person from the beginning of the relationship, so your partner stopped feeling attracted to you. You're partner does not feel they are with the same person they initially started dating.

This might be a little hard to grasp, so I'm going to put it in another perspective. Let's say you're a guy and your girlfriend gains 300 pounds and is now humongous. You decide that you really don't like her anymore because she is so overweight and you break up with her. She then yells and scream at you, and blames you for the break up. You think to yourself, me? No dear, you became incredibly overweight so I didn't find you attractive anymore. It's the same thing here! Your partner doesn't find *you* attractive anymore because certain qualities about you have changed.

Ultimately you need to look back on the relationship and figure out what about you (or your partner) changed, and **WHY** the break up took place. You may need third party help, so I encourage you to ask friends or family members (who knew both of you) their opinion on what they think happened, if you yourself cannot put a finger on it. While I can help you get your ex back with the techniques laid out in this book, we need to ultimately figure out WHY the break up occurred in order to **KEEP** our ex once we do get them back.

Chapter #2
The Break Up

"We need to talk"

Those words cut like a knife. It is one of the worst feelings to have the love of your life break up with you. Your partner says "I need space" or "we should just be friends" or maybe something else. The point is they want to end the relationship. You may have tried begging, apologizing, saying you love them, buying them gifts… **STOP RIGHT NOW**. I already told you these things actually *push* your ex away, and that hinders our progress.

Friend Zone

First off let me start by saying if your ex asks you to be just friends, **DENY THEM**. Tell them that you do not become friends with ex's (unless you cheated, then you need to be friends, but I will cover that later). You

see, the break up is hard on both
individuals, yes even your ex. So
when you agree to be friends,
you're actually making the break
up much easier for them. You're
remaining in contact with your
ex, comforting your ex, and
pretty much making the break up
an easier process for him or her,
until they can find another
partner."

The Relationship Has Already Ended

You've been dumped. Maybe it was yesterday, maybe a month ago, but it's over. You may have already made the mistakes of calling your ex, trying to "win" them back, telling your ex you love them, etc. Whatever you have done (as long as it's not too extreme) is OKAY, you can easily overcome these mistakes.

So what's the first thing you should do here? Well, probably the opposite of what you have been doing. The first thing you need to do is **LET YOUR EX GO**. Yes I said it, let the break up happen! There's a lot of psychology behind this, but you need to let your ex go before they will ever want to come back. Let's go over this a little.

I know it may be hard, but you have to come to grasp with this; when someone has broken up with you, they no longer like you and to the point where they no longer want to be in a relationship with you. Basically anything you do at this point is going to push them away even further and dissipate any feelings they have left for you even more. Your ex needs to feel like they lost you before they will ever want you back. It is only after they feel they have truly "lost" you, can these feelings come back. Why is this? Because people want what they can't have. It's the psychology 101, and it is real. This "lost" feeling is temporary though. If after you get back together you are the same person as when the two of you broke up, then the break up will happen again rather quickly. We will discuss how to become the person you were when you initially started dating later in the book.

So how do you make your ex feel like they lost you? Send them a letter. You could use email or text, but I recommend you don't and use a letter. The reason why is because it's unconventional and more intimate. There is more of an emotional connection with a hand written letter.

Keep your letter short. Put in your letter that you were acting a little crazy before (if you were, such as sending your ex non-stop texts, constantly telling him or her how much you love them, etc.) and that you completely agree with the break up. Tell your ex you think the break up is the best for both of you and you wish them luck in life. Do not tell them they are gross, a bitch, or anything of that nature. You have to keep things friendly for later. Here's an example for a female who has been broken up with:

Dear Robert,

I just wanted to say I was acting a little crazy before. And you know what, you're absolutely right, we should be broken up. I'm starting to date other people and this break up is the best thing for both of us.

- Jessica

You're thinking that's crazy! Why would I tell my ex, the person I love, that I don't want to be with them anymore? As we just went over, people want what they cannot have, and you become "gone." So look here, you're gone, you're no longer available, and you're soon going to become "unobtainable" in their eyes. With that being said, when you send this email or letter, you cannot go back to your old ways. You have to mean what you wrote or do enough acting to where they actually believe, "Wow, this person is gone for good. They really don't want me anymore. Maybe we shouldn't have broken up. Where are they going? Are they gone forever? Are they dating someone else? I miss them. I want them back!"

You see, what you're doing here is actually turning the tables on your ex. It's almost as if after they broke up with you, you broke up with them. Talk about your ex-partner being confused! Just this trick alone may be enough for them to re-establish contact with you.

What If My Partner Has Not Yet Broken Up With Me

Sometimes you just have a gut feeling things aren't working out. You may be thinking your partner is about to drop the bomb on you. If this is the case then I'm sorry, but it's *too late* to fix the problem. No secret lines or roses are going to bring back the attraction your partner had for you when you initially started dating. However, you can stack the deck in your favor here. And I want you to know, what you're about to do is temporary. You're just planting a seed so your flower (aka your relationship) can grow again. Okay, so here is what you need to do... break up with your partner first.

WHAT?

Yes, it may seem elementary, but it plants a huge seed in their mind. He or she may have been planning on breaking up with you but when you leave them, there is an actual chemical change in their brain to "get you back." So go through with the entire break up. Tell your partner that you need space and the relationship wasn't working. Do not get angry, frustrated, or emotional, even if they do. You must stay calm, and really act like you do not want to date them anymore. This is **very** important.

Chapter #3
The Most Important Rule of All

This rule by itself may have your ex crawling back. This rule alone could solve all your problems. This rule is the most important and imperative rule in this book. This rule IS hard to follow. I admit, I have broken it before, but I wish I hadn't. This rule is important, and I can't stress that enough. What's this super important, imperative, crazy, awesome rule you're wondering...

The "No Contact" Rule

It's exactly how it sounds... you cannot contact your ex for at least 30 days after you have provided them the hand written letter or email we went over in the last chapter. You may be thinking "but if I don't contact my ex for that long they'll forget all about me." Come on now, you probably still remember your first grade teacher, and you never dated her (I hope). You're still on your ex's mind and they will still remember you.

There are many reasons for this "no contact" rule. One is simple, you are no longer contacting your ex, and they will miss you. Sure he or she broke up with you for a certain reason, but they stayed with you for other reasons. Think about it, a week ago you were talking to your partner every day and you're about to cut them off cold turkey… they **WILL** be confused. As the weeks go on, your ex gets lonelier and sadder. They start reminiscing on the relationship. The longer time goes by, the more they remember the good times and forget the bad ones.

Many times with the no contact rule, your ex will contact **YOU**. This is obviously a great sign and I will show you how to handle this later in the book. Oh and when I say no contact, I'm talking about not contacting your ex, *as well as* their friends, family, co-workers, or anybody else they knows. You cannot phone up one of their friends and ask how your ex is doing. You know your ex will find out and this ruins all your progress! Remember, you are "gone."

What this "no contact" rule does is gives you and your partner a little break from each other. Right when the break up happens emotions are tense and the relationship is heated. When you say "okay" and give your partner a break, it gives you both time to step back and look at the big picture. This also makes you appear mature, calm, cool, and collective; all attractive qualities.

By the way, these 4 weeks are not wasted time. You will be using them, as I explain later in the next few chapters, to "restore" yourself so you become attractive to your ex again.

Chapter #4
Make a Plan

Make a plan; I think this is the second most important rule in the book, if I'm the judge here. Without a plan, this whole system will fall apart. The first thing to do is obtain some type weekly planner or use the calendar on your phone. Now mark with an X the day you calmly agreed to end the relationship by providing your ex the break up letter. Then I want you to count 30 days from this point, and place another X in your calendar. I think you see where I'm going with this. That second X is when you will be contacting your ex not one day before that; I mean it, don't contact them! However, if they contact you, there are a whole another set of rules to follow which I will show you later in this book.

The rest of your calendar will involve improving yourself, which you will read more about in the next chapter. From haircuts, to work out days, put it all on your calendar and stick to your plan; this is very important.

Chapter #5
Restoring Yourself

Okay time to pick yourself back up, easy right? Trust me, I know it's not easy. Sadness is obviously normal; the love of your life just broke up with you. If you find yourself in a depressed slump which would include never wanting to get out of bed, crying constantly, etc., and find you are "stuck," I would seriously recommend seeing a counselor or psychologist. I can say from personal experience that just talking to someone about a break up and life in general can help a ton. Of course, the best way to pick yourself up is to remain busy doing things and leading a purposeful life. I'll give you some techniques to help you do this later in the book.

Okay you've provided your ex with the breakup letter, and now you're implementing the no contact rule, great! These steps are hard but very necessary in the long run. You have 30 days (or less if your ex contacts you). You need to use these 30 days wisely. So first and foremost, you need to delete all memories of your ex. I would suggest writing all this information down, giving it to someone, and telling them to hide it somewhere for you.

- *Delete their phone number from your phone.*

- *Hide any pictures of your ex or the two of you together.*

- *Hide any gifts they may have given you.*

- *Do **NOT** delete them from your Facebook or Snapchat (I'll explain later). However hide their profile and stop following them.*

- *Make sure you DO change your Facebook status to single.*

The fewer reminders of your ex, the better; it makes this process 100 times easier.

Okay, so here is the mindset you should have right now, "My ex broke up with me, but it's okay. I can easily find another partner. There are plenty of people in this world. If we get back together after 30 days great; if not, oh well, life goes on." If you truly keep this mindset, it will show when you talk/meet with your ex again. How you appear to your ex after the break up can easily make or break getting back together with them. If you seem needy and eager to get back with them, you will push them away **FAST**. Remember you just said you agreed with the breakup and it was a good thing... so mean it! If you come off as busy, moved on, and enjoying life, your ex will notice the changes.

Okay so now that you're in the right mindset you can start working on yourself. The first date at the end of these 30 days is what I call the "re-attraction" date. You're igniting a new spark, you're a new person. You're not the same person from the old relationship, you're new, you're fresh, you're fun.

All In Your Head

You have collected yourself at this point, and your emotions are calmer. The first thing you need to do is take a look at the whole situation; step back and take a look at the real relationship. Many times, even when people we don't like sweep the rug out from under us, we all of a sudden "want them back" because they are no longer obtainable.

I'm sure you have been in a situation where you didn't like a person much, but then they stopped talking to you, or maybe you saw them out with another person, and all of a sudden you needed to have them. This is something I like to call "all in your head". It's just your brain playing tricks on you. So take a step back, and go over the positives and negatives of your ex in your head.

For a relationship to last, you really want to find someone who shares many of the same beliefs and values as you. If you don't have things in common, or there are too many differences between the two of you, it can be a troubling relationship and a different partner may be a better match. Whoever said "opposites attract" had never been in a very good relationship.

The first thing to work on is your appearance. Though your personality is a huge factor, the first thing people notice is how you look. Maybe your clothes are a little on the old side? Maybe you could lose a little weight? Maybe your teeth could be a little whiter? You don't need much money to improve yourself. I want you to take a look in the mirror and say, "What can I do to improve myself?"

This is not changing who you are at all, that's not what we're going for here. You're just improving your appearance. You need to appear new, fresh, classy, and improved, like the break up **REALLY** was the best thing for you. Just think, you're out somewhere and maybe one of your ex's friends sees the new you; you know they will tell your ex. What do you want them to say? "Hey I just saw Courtney. Oh man, good thing you dumped her ass. She looked like she just rolled outta bed.".... Or would you rather them say something like, "Hey I just saw Courtney. Wow she's looking so good! Can you give me her number... it's been long enough to ask for that right?"

Choice two, DUH!

Next thing to do is change all those bad qualities that you may have started acquiring. Think back on before you started dating your partner:

- *Who were you?*
- *Have you changed?*
- *Did any of your qualities become "unattractive"?*

You have 30 days to bring back your "attractive" side, so use them. You could begin by restarting that hobby that you let go because you became so preoccupied with your partner. You could reconnect with friends you may have bailed on because your partner took up all your time. The point is to get your life back! Your life did not revolve around this person before you started dating them, nor should it ever, dating them or not. It's YOUR life, they are now a part of it too when you are in a relationship.

Chapter #6
Play the Field

Okay, this part may seem counter intuitive but it really can build massive amounts of jealousy... start talking other people and play the field. "Look at Rob, he's with another girl. He no longer wants me. Does he even think about me anymore? Should I have broken up with him? Wow she's pretty. Wow, he's no longer available. I WANT HIM SO BAD!" Remember, you're "gone." Your ex can no longer have you. Then throw in a little jealousy if you're out with another person, and emotions really start escalating.

So here's my advice... go out on dates and have fun. This does not have to be serious. You're going on dates with other people, maybe hooking up with them if you'd like. You're having fun and enjoying life; if you end up actually dating another person, great. Who knows, they may be better than your ex! The objective here is to feel better about yourself and if you start talking to the opposite sex, you will feel better about yourself. You'll feel happier, and be in higher spirits knowing you can get other partners and your ex just becomes another option. Plus, word will most likely get around that you are out with other people which will bring out jealousy in your ex.

Needing and Wanting

When you are trying to get your ex back, you can want him or her back, but you cannot need him or her back. People have a six sense for this sort of thing. When you need your ex back, they know they can do anything they want and you will always be there. When you want your ex back, they become an option, which changes everything. You can become "gone." This is why playing the field is so important. When you widen your selection, your ex becomes "just another option." Keep this mindset and it will show on the first date.

Jealousy is one of the biggest emotions you can provoke. You used to be theirs you know, and even if they broke up with you, jealousy provokes a range of emotions. Knowing this, we can use it to our advantage with social media.

Chapter #7
Social Media

Social media can actually be quite advantageous for us when it comes to getting our ex back, and can be a good tool to use. First, keep your ex as your Facebook and Snapchat friend but do not look at their profile. I repeat do not look at their profile. I cannot stress this enough. Guess what looking at their profile will do... destroy your emotions!

You might see that other people are talking to your ex, or that they are dating someone, or that their friends are making fun of you. You might get angry, act impulsively, break the no contact rule and message your ex. This will **DESTROY** your chances of ever getting them back. So just do not look at their profile. I would even suggest unfollowing them and hiding all posts or stories from them, so there are absolutely no reminders of your ex.

Now hopefully you have already changed your relationship status to single. If you haven't, go change it to single **RIGHT NOW**. Leaving it as "in a relationship" or putting up that even more awkward "its complicated" like a pre-teen middle schooler will not bring your ex back.

Something else I see quite often is the "weeping status updates." Please do not do this! No depressing song lyrics, no "you'll think of me", or "you'll regret this." Statuses like this do not help your situation. Just leave your status blank for a while, or if you do change it, make sure it's happy. Put something positive you're doing, like how much fun you're going to have that night. Make something up if you have to, just make sure it's nothing sad or depressing!

So you're single, which indicates you're looking for another partner, awesome. You're doing great. Start going out and when you do, make sure to put in your status what you're doing, especially if you're going places with members of the opposite sex. Take pictures with groups of people, at parties, events, etc. You're doing great, your life is great, you could care less about your ex. Make sure to update your story on Snapchat too especially if you're out somewhere or with a member of the opposite sex.

I want you to trust me here, your ex will find out. It may not seem like it, but I can guarantee you they will at some point look at your Facebook and Snapchat as long as you stay Facebook and Snapchat friends with them, I promise.

So what is going on here? You're making yourself look popular and wanted. You're showing your ex how well things are going for you, and that you have moved on. As in you were telling the truth in your letter, and you no longer need or want them. This is turn will create an emotional response with your ex in the form of jealousy. Jealousy is a very strong emotion in humans, and could be greatly heightened if you were to start seeing someone else.

The New Partner Technique

While just being in pictures with the opposite sex may stir up emotions with your ex, you can do something which will make them immediately start thinking about your relationship together, and regret their decision of breaking up with you. Again, your ex was once yours, and even if they broke up with you they still have feelings for you; feelings that you can get back.

This technique may not be for everyone, however I can say with confidence that this technique is **EXTREMELY EFFECTIVE**, and I want you to seriously consider trying it. I've seen this work so many times when couples have separated from each other. The reason why is, all humans share similar characteristics. We all respond to certain stimuli. We cry when we are sad, our stomachs growl when we get hungry, we scratch ourselves when we itch. These are all unlearned responses that humans partake in from stimuli. Human jealousy, which is a psychological emotion in humans, also has a stimuli. You see, when something, or someone, that a human being once had becomes someone else's, they get jealous. Knowing all this, we can and should use it to our advantage by portraying that we are in a relationship with someone else.

What?

You heard that right. The reason for this is because it brings an enormous amount of jealously out in your ex, especially if they are not with someone themselves. They recently broke up with you and are expecting you to be begging for them back... but you're not. You're already with someone else! This doesn't make any sense to them. Then they will start replaying their decision in their mind. All the negative aspects of you start going away, and they start to only remember the positive aspects of you. They start thinking to themselves things like, should I have broken up with her? I thought he liked me? I can't have her anymore? I want him back!

Now you can't *actually* start dating someone else, as that would be too complicated. What you are going to create a profile on a dating app such as Tinder, and put in the bio that you are looking for a fake boyfriend/girlfriend for a week. A good idea is to offer an incentive in the bio in order to make it worth their while. An example being you'll take them out for dinner or to a movie for free in exchange for their help.

It may surprise you, but you will get quite a few people who will take you up on this offer. When you meet this person, I want you to take a number of pictures with them in all different situations. I want you to post on your Snapchat story with them, and upload pictures of the two of you to Facebook. I want you to make it look like you are already talking to someone else, and could be potentially dating this person soon.

I know this may seem weird, or maybe a little crazy, but if you truly want your ex back, this technique works! As stated, jealousy is a very strong emotion in humans and one that can bring back all sorts of feelings for you with your ex. This can make them immediately regret their decision, and really is the quickest way to get them back. Don't be surprised if your ex starts texting you within a few days of you "dating" this new person.

Again, I know this all may seem out there, but this really works, which is why I'm including here in this book. If you decide to go this route, you need to adhere to one important rule:

Do Not Tell Anyone You're Doing This
Think about if people found out you have a fake boyfriend or girlfriend to try and make your ex jealous, it wouldn't go over too well. Tell absolutely no one you are doing this; no one. This will be our secret.

This technique can get you back with your ex fast, however going back to your old ways can cause you to break up all over again. As stated in Chapter 1, you have to really think about why the break up occurred and change the aspects of yourself that made it happen. You don't just want your ex back temporarily; you want to keep them back! For this reason you need to look at the big picture of why the break up happened in the first place.

So what should you do if your ex starts talking to you again after you use this technique? Take it very slow. Wait a while to answer their texts or calls. Say no to hanging out. You need them to really start missing you. As they continue being in contact with you, slowly start speaking to them again. Chapter 10 goes into more detail on what to do on the first date, however just remember take things slow!

Think of it as slowly walking into a pool and the water slowly comes up your body with each step you take. You are not jumping into the pool. The slower you go, the better things will be. It's like you're meeting your ex again for the first time. Think about all those sparks going around when you first started talking. Then as things progress, break up with your "new" girlfriend/boyfriend and never bring it up with anyone. If your ex asks, just say it's in the past and change the subject.

Chapter #8
They're Dating Someone Else

If they are dating someone else, not all techniques discussed before will be the same. I could write another book on this subject, but I will include it all right here.

Ouch! This hurts I know, but in no way is this the end of the rope. When you figure out they are dating someone else, a gut reaction is to call your ex and tell him or her how much you hate them, how gross they are, but don't do that. This will only push your ex further into the arms of their new partner and not help you one bit. Instead, don't do anything. Do the opposite of what you think you should do. Do not call your ex, do not text your ex, do not talk to your ex's friends. The point here is to not let your ex know you even think about them. They've moved on, or so they say, so you have to be double moved on, you get my drift? You have to care less than they do.

What does this do? This makes you look extremely confident and attractive to your ex. You are no longer fixated on them, begging for them back. You're talking to other girls/guys, you have moved on, you're "gone." After the first fight with their new partner, they'll start thinking about you again.

A fun fact is rebound relationships rarely ever last. The average time for a rebound relationship is 2-5 weeks. They just don't work. They are rushed, spontaneous, and die out quick. And think, if your ex rushed that quickly into a relationship, they still have feelings for you they are just trying to bury. The 30 day no contact rule still applies here, unless their new partner breaks up with your ex before that. That is your time to move in. Your ex will be heartbroken and will look for a familiar, comforting face, and you can be there for them. However you must still take it slow still. (Please read the end of "first date" section of this book to know what take it slow means, this is important.)

What If My Ex and Their New Partner Don't Break Up

You can still get your ex back, but you're going to have to wait a little longer. Drop out of sight by implementing the "no contact" rule. Start working on yourself like I discussed before. Now let me give you a brief overview on new relationships.

New Relationships

For new relationships, the beginning is something I like to call the "honeymoon phase." It can last from a few days to a little over a month. There is nothing you can say or do to pull your ex away from this awesome, amazing, and fun person (or so their emotions tell them). However after a little while, this "new relationship spark" ends up dying out. They start annoying each other, they've talked about everything, they're not having as much fun… and they start fighting.

So when you believe this "honeymoon phase" has ended is the time you should move in. I would recommend waiting at least 30 days after your ex and their partner have gotten together. And I'm sorry to do this to you, but when I say move in, I mean as "just a friend." I know, I know, I'm putting you in the friend zone. But it is just for a little while, and I promise I will get you out of it.

So now what? Be there for them. You're their friend. At first you are going to have to contact them more, ask them how their days going, send them a funny e-mail, and just be around in their life. Don't be creepy now, don't text or call them too much. You're their friend, not their stalker. If they don't text you back one day, whatever, don't get mad. You should be their sounding board. If they have a problem with their life, be there to listen, even if it is about their new partner. Don't offer any advice on how to solve problems with their new partner; you're just a sounding board at this point.

You've established a friendship with your ex, now what? Now is the time you have to become Houdini. What I mean is disappear a little, but not completely. If they text you, don't text them back right away. Skip an email. Call them back the next day. Become unavailable and busy. They will get curious, jealous, and a whole slew of other emotions. Then after a little while of this call them and ask them to lunch. Something like, "Well I'm pretty busy tomorrow, but how bout we get lunch on Saturday around noon?" Then read the first date portion of this book to learn how to re-ignite attraction. If you successfully "re-ignite" this attraction, they will want to ditch their new partner and get back with you! You will start talking more, being together more, and eventually they will leave their partner for you. Just remember to take it slow, and recall the "Why They Broke Up With Me" chapter so it does not happen again.

Chapter #9
What If You Cheated

————————————

You cheated… you ass hole! Just kidding. I myself have been unfaithful before and I know the experience. People make mistakes! Now if this is your 15th time cheating, you might have a problem. But if not, you can get your ex back.

Why Did You Cheat

Listen, you didn't cheat for the hell of it. Your relationship may have had some problems. Maybe you lost interest in your ex. Maybe the person you cheated on your ex with was more fun. Maybe you were fighting with your ex a lot. This may be hard to grasp, but you could just want your ex back now because, as I said before, when someone leaves us there is a chemical change in the brain to "get them back." It is almost as if no one else could fill their shoes. So all the good memories flood your mind and you seem to forget all the bad ones. For example, you remember how hot they looked in the backseat of your car or how their hair blows in the wind, but you seem to forget the all the times you two fought or how they eat their boogers at the dinner table. The point is you cheated for a reason, and I want you to seriously think to yourself:

- *Do I really want my ex back?*
- *Why did I cheat?*
- *Do I really want to put in the time and effort to rebuild the "trust" I just lost?*

After you have *seriously* looked over these options, and if you decide you really do want your ex back, here is your plan. We will start with the "do not" list.

DO NOT

- *Buy Them Gifts*
- *Text Message Them Constantly*
- *Push Them To Make A Decision*
- *Call Them*
- *E-Mail Them*
- *Stalk Them*
- *Get Desperate and Needy*
- *Panic*
- *Say Sorry a Million Times*
- *Tell Them You'll Change*

You may have already done some of the things on the list above, but it is okay. You now understand that these things do not work and you need to stop immediately. So here is what you should do. The first thing you need to do is let your ex scream. They will scream and yell and cry and you need to sit there and nod. Do not say anything yet, just listen. After they are done ranting make one sincere, heartfelt apology. If you are not face to face, I want you to write a letter. You need to be sincerely sorry. Here is an example:

Dear Jessica,

I know what you're feeling right now. I can't believe I did this but it will never happen again. I know this is all my fault and I am truly sorry. Please forgive me Jessica.

With All My Heart,
Robert

Here are things you must do when you apology:

- **You Have To Accept The Blame** - *Do not make excuses, even if you think it was their fault. Just take the blame for right now.*

- **You Have To Apologize** - *One sincere heartfelt apology will go much longer than 1 million "I'm sorry's".*

- **You Have To Get Across That It Will Never Happen Again** - *You're trying to rebuild trust here. Sure they'll blow you off because they are so furious, but they will remember that you said that it won't happen again and that you're sorry.*

Now that you have said sorry, allow the breakup to happen! I repeat, let them break up with you! It is necessary in this case. You have to build the trust back up before they will ever accept you again. Trying to crawl back to your ex too early will amplify bad feelings and push them away. Instead, just as the musical artists the Black Eyed Peas once said, you're going to meet them halfway.

So you have said sorry and have allowed the breakup to happen, now what? **CEASE CONTACT**. Minimum here is a week. It might not make sense to you but it is crucial. If your ex tries to contact you, ignore it. The point here is to get your ex to miss you again and almost regret breaking up with you because you're now gone. You being "gone" in their mind will create a great amount of attraction because they will "want you back." They may contact you the first couple days and say something like "Well do you have anything to say?" Your gut reaction would be to say something like, "I'm sooo sorry", "I love you", Blah Blah Blah, **STOP**. You need to ignore this text, or phone call, or however your ex contacts you.

Don't worry about losing them to someone else this soon. They are not over you at all, and they still care and think about you. Plus, if your ex is dating some other person within a week they are not a good person and I wouldn't date them anyway (I'm kidding, but seriously what person would be with someone else within a week?)

After a week, contact your ex and keep things light. Do not bring up the cheating at all. If they say anything about the cheating, let them know your apology was sincere and then change the subject. Suggest a casual lunch or maybe coffee on a day that you know will be convenient for them. This will be like a first date again. Please refer to "first date" chapter at the end of this book to learn how to complete this process.

Chapter #10
Restoring Contact

A number of things can happen during the 4 weeks of "no contact." One of ex's friends might call you, maybe your ex sends you some texts, or maybe you don't hear anything from them. Here is your plan for all of these scenarios:

What If One of Their Friends Contact You Before 4 Weeks is Over

Okay, so one of their friends tries calling you up or texting you. You're probably really curious what they have to say, so go ahead and answer that call. See what they have to say. Keep this call short, less than a minute or two, and do not bring up anything about the relationship. **DO NOT** ask how your ex is doing. Do not bring up anything about your ex. You want to use this as an opportunity to explain how great your life is going and how the break-up was for the best.

Then you're going to bring up the "new person" you're seeing. Make it seem like you didn't want them to know, like it slipped out. Now most likely you won't be seeing a "new person" but this little white lie can have a huge impact when your ex finds out. Your ex's friend may make up some lame excuse but the only real reason they're friend is talking to you is to be your ex's little spy.

What If Your Ex Contacts You Before the 4 Weeks is Over

YES, this is the best possible scenario. It may have been the next day, it may have been three weeks later. This is irrelevant, the main point is your ex thought about you enough to actually call or text you. Most likely he or she may just ask how you're doing. Listen to this part very carefully, you **CANNOT** take them back fully just yet. Let's say your ex calls you and asks how you're doing. You must seem happy and busy. You can say something like:

> *"Oh hey Robert, great to hear from you. Hey can I call you back later, I'm kind of busy right now."*

You can change this a little, you can make a little small talk, but you cannot be on the phone for more than 2-3 minutes. Also, you cannot bring up anything about the relationship; nothing about the past, not yet. You have moved on, remember? This same rule applies if they text you. Just replace "call back later" with "text back later."

What does this do? Well they see that you have moved on. You're making them wait for you; you're putting them second to your busy life (something you may not have done when you dated them). Your ex is no longer a part of your life and this will bring out a wide variety of emotions and get them thinking about you.

Next thing to do is hold off on that call or text. Get back to your ex much later on in the day or even the next day. This part is hard but essential. Again, keep the call short, make small talk, and try to let your ex lead the conversation. Do **NOT** act angry, sad, rude, bring up anything about the relationship, brag about all the people you've been with, or ask what people *they've* been with! You are calm, happy, and moved on. Then make sure you are the first to say "got to go" and hang up!

If your ex happens to bring up anything about the relationship, you can talk about it, but don't act desperate; stay calm and collected. Just listen to them talk and if they say something like "can we give it another shot" or asks you out on a date, you can say yes but it has to be under certain conditions. You want them to have to work to get **YOU** back, so have your ex do something nice for you. An example would be having them pick you up for the date.

What If Your Ex Does Not Contact You

Do not worry if your ex doesn't contact you. Some girls/guys will not call for one reason or another, but may very well have wanted to. So you have waited the 30 days, you have restored yourself, you're confident, and you have played the field. If you have done all this correctly I salute you. All these items will greatly increase your chances of getting your ex back.

Now it's been a long time since you last contacted your ex. If you give them a call out of the blue, they might answer… but they might not. Seeing your name on their caller ID could bring up a variety of emotions and they may choose to let your call go. Then you have to leave a voicemail and things get a little more complicated. The best thing that could happen would be your ex answering their phone and talking to you. I have found setting the phone call up with a text message beforehand gives you the greatest chance of getting an answer.

What you want to do here is send your ex a text with a purpose. A text with a purpose is much more likely to get a response than something like "what's up" or "how you doing". Then when they respond back to your message, you can say you need more help and ask to call them "about it" later, which sets up your phone call. A great example of a text message with a purpose would be sending your ex a text about a subject they may have known a lot about which you want some "advice" on. Let's say your ex was a health nut and knew a lot about vitamins and supplements. And let's say you would like to know some good supplements to take for boosting energy. An example text would be:

"Hey Jessica. I know it's been a little while, but I'm having some problems with energy and was seeing if I can call you later to ask you some questions about supplements."

Then after your ex responds, set up the phone call for a time later on at night. Tell them you'll be free later at a specific time, and that you'll call them around then. Make sure it's a time they will most likely be free too. After your ex has agreed to the phone call, say something like:

"Okay cool. I'm gonna be free around 8PM later. I'll call you then."

If they are busy during this time, ask them when they'll be free and call them then. Do **not** flirt with your ex or put any smiley faces in these first text messages. You do not want to show any type of interest right now. Also, do **not** ask your ex on a date during these text messages. You are just trying to initiate contact between the two of you. Asking your ex on a date is reserved for the phone call when they will be more likely to agree to it. Considering you have just texted them (which breaks the contact barrier), and you set up a specific time you are going to be calling them, you are giving yourself the best chance of them answering your phone call versus a cold call out of nowhere.

When you do call your ex, ask them how they're doing, get that "advice" you needed, and then get to talking! You want to have a fun conversation with them. If you're not the smoothest on the phone, write some things down on a pad before you call. This way if the conversation gets stale, you can quickly look at the pad and bring up a new topic. Some great topics to talk about would be rumors about people you both know, recent news events, jokes you can both laugh at, and reminiscing on times when you both shared a fun experience together. You want to stimulate your ex's emotions and get them thinking about you again.

After you feel you've had a solid conversation, say "I got to go." This is important; you want to make sure you're the first to get off the phone and **leave them**. This will make them want more. Then hang up.

You have broken the contact barrier and contact has been established; this is good. Now you are going to wait a week to text them again. Here is another situation where they may contact you within this week since you have broken the contact barrier. But if they don't, wait a week and then just send them a text asking something casual, such as how their week has been. You are now taking things slowwwwwww. Very slow. Slower than you think. You need to have your ex come back to you, you are **not** chasing your ex. Think of this like it's the first time meeting your ex, think about how slow you would have taken things. As the weeks progress, you can text more, and talk on the phone. Things should get better in terms of a connection. Then when you feel enough communication has been established, you can set up the "first date."

This is going to be the first date you have with your ex since the break up. You want to do this over the phone and not via text. The phone is more personable and you have a better chance of getting a yes response. Casual is something like coffee or ice cream somewhere, not dinner or a movie. Remember you're busy, so say it is going to be short because you have to be somewhere (you can make up something, your ex doesn't know your life anymore). Then end the phone call. An example would be:

Robert: *Hey Jessica, what are you up to?*

Jessica: *(Response)*

Robert: *(Talk for a little while and then...) Hey I got to go, I'm about to go eat dinner. It was fun talking to you Jessica.*

Jessica: *(Response)*

Robert: *Hey it's been a little while though, we should catch up. I'm busy tomorrow, but you want to meet up at Starbucks for a drink on Tuesday night?*

Jessica: *(Response)*

Robert: *Okay, I'll text you tomorrow to let you know an exact time. Talk to ya later.*

That is all you need. Now don't tell them too much in this phone call. You want to create a sense of mystery about yourself. They have not talked to you in a month or maybe longer; you're new to them, fresh… let their mind wander. And in all honesty, if you talk too long the conversation could get boring which will not help your ex agree to that date!

What If Your Ex Doesn't Answer Anything?

In the worst case scenario, your ex does not answer your texts or calls. If this is the case, you are going to have to let things go for a while. The more you text and call them without an answer, the more you end up pushing them away. The best strategy for this type of situation is to wait it out another month and then try to re-establish contact again. Bring up a time you guys had a lot of fun and connected, such as a concert or comedy club you went to together. This will bring up positive emotions in your ex, get them thinking about you, and will be your best chance at evoking a response. Then just follow my advice from before, and try to get them to start chasing you. Make sure you are using all the tools brought up in this book.

I will re-iterate it here, you have to get your ex to come back to you. You *cannot* chase your ex back, as this does not work.

Chapter #11
The First Date

You got a date with your ex! Hopefully you picked some place casual for interesting conversation; coffee is my favorite. The whole point of this date is to "re-ignite" the attraction your ex had for you. He or she liked you **a lot** at one time. It was when you two first met, when you were new to each other, interesting, fun. This is when you can be that all over again. The key to this date is to keep things light, fun, and interesting. Do not (unless they do) bring up anything about your past relationship, **do not**. This is very important.

On this first date there a few things you want to do. First off you want to appear changed, as in the "new you," so hopefully you have worked on yourself as I explained in the previous chapter.

Now like I said before, you don't want to bring up anything about the previous relationship during this date. If however, your ex starts talking about the break-up, let them talk a little and then say, "I don't want to talk about the past right now; it's the past. Let's just have fun tonight" and change the subject. If they continue pressing on about your past relationship, just listen to them talk and then say, "I understand your feelings and we can discuss this all another time, let's just not do it now."

The next thing to remember is to keep this date short. You're busy and have a great life; you just met to catch up. This date can be no more than an hour max. Make sure you are the first to say that you have to go. This time you're leaving, not your ex, and this will spark attraction. At the end of the date do not schedule another date; you want to give that a little time. If however your ex asks you to go somewhere or schedules another date, it's okay to say yes.

After this date, it is very likely you will start talking to your ex again and hopefully be back together with them soon. Again, make sure to take things slow. If you try to jump back into the relationship too fast you can end up pushing your ex away again. So take it slow, slower than you think you should. Wait a week or so before trying to ask them out on another date. If your ex asks you on another date, you can accept but try to pick the place you two are going so you seem like the one in control. A great second date is going to a park and looking at nature, the stars, and just talking, or going to a fun event like a concert; you want emotions for each other flowing again. One exception to this "slow rule" is getting sexual with your partner. You want to get sexual again as soon as possible! The reason for this is because kissing, cuddling, and anything else sexual is bonding for couples and brings them closer together.

> **Fact**: When two people go thru an emotionally elevated experience it bonds them together. Bonding happens subconsciously through shared experiences.

Do not bring up getting back into a relationship for a while, especially because they very well may say it first. As you feel things getting better, and you and your ex become comfortable again, you can **THEN** progress things into a relationship. When you get back together, remember my advice and don't fall into the same patterns that caused this break-up in the first place.

To maintain your relationship for the long run, keep up your appearance and keep the relationship exciting for you and your partner; this keeps their interest maintained for the long term. You don't want to be farting next to them on the couch again. One way to keep your relationship fun is to go on a "date night" at least once a month. Here are some great example dates:

- Couples massage
- Bike rides
- Mini golf
- Ice skating
- Board games
- Theatre plays
- Boating
- Sharing a bubble bath
- Romantic scavenger hunt
- Visiting local attractions
- Weekend getaways
- Visiting art galleries
- Pretend house hunting
- Comedy clubs
- Wine bar
- Bowling
- The Zoo
- Sporting events

I was out at a wine bar the other night and I noticed a married older couple. They had to be in their late sixties and they were all over each other, kissing and enjoying wine. They were laughing and having fun. I thought to myself, wow, now that's how relationships should be! Who knows how long they'd been together, but yet they still kept the relationship alive! You want to do the same.

Remember to have your own life and continue to be yourself. Get hobbies, hang out with old friends, and find something you're passionate about to pursue in life. You can be with your boyfriend or girlfriend, but do not make your life about your boyfriend or girlfriend. Give each other space from time to time. Space is good for relationships as it causes both partners to miss each other. Keep the relationship fresh. Be someone your partner wants to be with.

If you are enjoying this book, could you please leave a review on Amazon? It would be greatly appreciated and allow me to come out with more informative books in the future. A shortened link to the review page is below:

linkpony.com/blueprint

Conclusion

I hope you've learned a great deal of knowledge from this book. When you do end up getting back into a relationship, make sure to show you care about your partner. Take time to find out about how their day went, even if it's just for a few minutes. Be physically affectionate by giving them hugs, kisses, back rubs, etc. Give each other space from time to time to let each other breathe. Forgive each other and try to let go of the past when needed.

Even if you make every right move, some relationships cannot be saved. All circumstances are different, and every relationship is unique. Learn from your mistakes and live life. You want to be happy in your relationship, not exhausted from trying to get the approval of your partner. You need to be happy. I truly do believe that everything in life happens for a reason. If you remember this, then everything will be okay.

Need extra help? Have a unique situation? If after reading this book you would like personal assistance from me, please go to the VIP section on my website, which can be found at GetMoreDates.com. The website also contains additional books and articles I have written related to relationships.

◆　◆　◆

If you enjoyed this book, you may also like...

The Art of The Text
The Ultimate Guide on Texting Girls

Shortened Link to Book:
linkpony.com/text

Do you struggle texting girls? Are your texts not getting responses? Don't know the right things to say? In The Art of The Text, Zac Miller takes your hand and shows you exactly what to text girls to have them begging to be with you! From getting her number to the first date, it's all included in this book. Learn how to text girls today!

How to Attract Women
The Last of the Dating Books You'll Ever Need

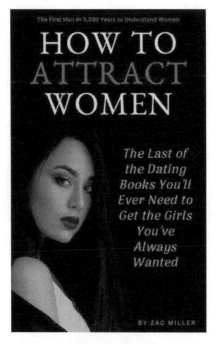

Shortened Link to Book:
linkpony.com/attract

Girls have been a mystery for thousands of years however one man has finally figured them out. In *How to Attract Women*, author Zac Miller goes over the entire process of attracting women. Appearance, conversation topics, psychological techniques, body language, and much more... it's all included in this book! **You can** be with the girl of your dreams! Find out how by going to the link above!

MATCHED
How to Get Girls on Tinder, Bumble, or Any Other Dating App or Website

Shortened Link to Book
linkpony.com/match

Struggling when it comes to getting girls on dating apps like Tinder & Bumble? Zac Miller has you covered! In his new book *MATCHED*, he goes over everything when it comes to getting girls on dating apps. The bio, the pictures, the messages, and the date - it's all covered! Find out more at the link above!

Made in the USA
Middletown, DE
30 July 2021